LETTERS
of the Heart

Blessings of Instinctive Humanitarianism

LEO MCGEE

ISBN 978-1-64670-890-1 (Paperback)
ISBN 978-1-64670-891-8 (Digital)

Covenant Books, Inc.
11661 Hwy 707
Murrells Inlet, SC 29576
www.covenantbooks.com

By Leo McGee

Letters of the Heart
Blessings of Instinctive Humanitarianism

Education of the Black Adult
An Historical Overview

Education of the Black Adult in the United States
An Annotated Bibliography

Lend an Ear
Heritage of the Upper Cumberland

Mini-Grants for Classroom Teachers

The Black Rural Landowner—Endangered Species
Social, Political, and Economic Implications

Dedication

This book is dedicated to those who, throughout the history of America, extended a hand of magnanimity to the oppressed. It is also dedicated to the oppressed who struggled mightily for survival and to make our great nation a better place for themselves and future generations.

PREFACE

Without a doubt, some of the most cherished moments of my youth was working in the yard of Mrs. Mary Conner in Crossett, Arkansas. Taking care of her yard was not work at all. Engrossed in the many yard and infrequent house tasks she assigned was my refuge—my heaven, far away from the mental abuse dished out to me in Colored Town at T.W. Daniel School. My peers preyed on my shortcomings—eyes out of sync, living in the country, lack of material resources, nine siblings. I never measured up, and they never let me forget it.

Mrs. Conner's approval of the tasks I accomplished came freely, warming my soul to the core. The meals she prepared especially for me touched me deeply. The kind words she spoke of my mother, who was her housekeeper, spoke of her humaneness. In my heart of hearts, I considered Mrs. Conner a Godsend. So did my mother.

After graduating in 1964 from Philander Smith College in Little Rock, I married my college sweetheart. Thereafter, we became teachers in the Chicago and Columbus, Ohio, school systems. On our returns to visit my mother, she always insisted that I visit Mrs. Conner.

Things changed! My mother informed me that Mr. Bob Conner, who was Director of Engineering for the Crossett Lumber Company, had accepted a job at Scotts Paper Company in Swarthmore, Pennsylvania. For more than fifteen years, I had no contact with Mrs. Conner except through conversations with my mother.

Then there was a letter in 1983! The exchange between Mrs. Conner and I continued until 2003—the renewal of a symbiotic relationship that spanned fifty years, 1953–2003!

The multifaceted story line of this book enhances its uniqueness. A quest for personal truth endeavored by the reader presents a favorable challenge—a gut check. There is no exacting theme. It is open to the reader's imagination.

THE
LETTERS

Tennessee Technological University
Cookeville, Tennessee

Memorandum

TO: Dr. Leo McGee, Assistant Dean, Extended Services
FROM: Larry D. Miller, Vice President for Development and
           Alumni Affairs
DATE: July 7, 1983
SUBJECT: Sunday at Heber Springs, AR

While attending a church service Sunday at the First Presbyterian Church in Heber Springs, Arkansas, with my recently widowed mother and my youngest son, a Mrs. Mary Conner Youngchild came up to me after service and asked me if I knew a Dr. Leo McGee. Of course, I denied my acquaintance with you—fearful that I might be implicated in some illegal scheme.

Mary explained to me that she knew you in Crossett, Arkansas, and had the highest compliments to make about you and your family. I told Mrs. Youngchild that we must be talking about two different people. She asked me to convey to you her fondest regards, and obviously, she was extremely proud of your accomplishments up to this point.

I have tried to call you several times, but you are either playing golf or your line is busy.

Please find enclosed the bulletin from the Sunday morning service in case you think I am making all this up.

JD
Enclosure

Tennessee Technological University
Cookeville, Tennessee

November 4, 1983

Mrs. Mary Conner Youngchild
C/O Rev. Dean T. Waychoff
First Presbyterian Church
1313 West Pine Street
Heber Springs, AR 72543

Dear Mrs. Youngchild:

Dr. Larry Miller of Tennessee Tech informed me that he made your acquaintance at the First Presbyterian Church in Heber Springs in July. I was delighted to learn of your whereabouts and that you are doing well.

It has been a long time since my days in your yard in Crossett. I got my most worthy lesson in discipline there. I also learned the real meaning of kindness. Simply put, I have always had the utmost appreciation for what you meant to me in my development and to my family.

I have two daughters. One is a freshman at the University of Tennessee and the other is in the sixth grade. My wife is from Helena and is a Tennessee Tech employee as well.

My brothers and sisters are scattered all over the country. My mother is doing fine and frequently speaks of you.

If you are ever traveling on Interstate Highway 40 in East Tennessee, please stop and visit.

Most cordially,
Leo McGee
Assistant Dean, Extended Services

Trout Haven
Wilburn Route 313
Heber Springs, Ark. 72543
November 13, 1983

Dear Leo,

How happy I was at church today to receive your letter. When Dr. Larry Miller told me he was from Cookeville, I thought of you immediately. Your mother has kept me up with you to some degree. Larry told me you were friends—at school and in Rotary. I told him you come from a very fine family and that I knew you as a young man.

Before I knew you were there, about 1974–5, Bob and I used to stop at Holiday Inn driving from Greenville, SC, back and forth to L Rock. I'll always remember Cookeville for that.

It's hard to believe that well over twenty years have passed since you and I were working in that yard together. Now that I'm months short of sixty-four, I do most of my work myself. I've even gone into vegetable gardening in my old age with a Troy Built Tiller, blue jeans, and muscle. Next year, I am cutting back because we have so much canned up ahead. In my retirement, I've worked as hard or harder than ever in my life. I've told your mother she'd be amazed to see me now.

I'll always remember meeting your Grandparents Lowe down at Safeway one day. Your granddad met my handshake with that hand that had taken so much suffering. He was a good, proud man, as was his wife, and his influence on your mother and on you was evident. He was a gentleman.

I was never able to get too close to your Dad until the day we had your sister's wedding at the church. Somehow, I felt much closer to him, and I felt he understood me better too.

I love your mother very much. I often wish I could have a visit with her. She did such a good job raising her children under circumstances that were not easy. I am happy to see her—as I did a few years ago—enjoying a far more leisurely life than she had ever known.

I am happy in a second marriage, tho' I'll never forget my dear Bob. It's better not to be alone, and Howard is a loving man.

We are on a trout river—Bob would never fish and I longed to. Now I have my own dock, a boat, and custom-made rods. I have a lot to tell Bob about what he missed.

I believe I met your wife at your sister's wedding. It's hard to believe you have a college freshman daughter—that's great—then a long wait for a second girl.

If I ever get back that way, I'll stop, but we haven't gone that way. In fact, we are in vacationland and don't go anywhere much.

My very best to you and yours,
Mary Conner Youngchild

Tennessee Technological University
Cookeville, Tennessee

November 25, 1983

Mrs. Mary Conner Youngchild
Wilburn Route 313
Heber Springs, AR 72543

Dear Mrs. Youngchild:

We have been in Cookeville for six years. I love it. My wife, Gloria, would rather be in Columbus, Ohio, or Nashville, where we have lived before—size of the cities, shopping malls and friends. By the way, she is from Helena, Arkansas. Both she and I work at Tennessee Tech. We have two daughters, Cassandra and Jennifer. My former boss at Ohio State University is president here. Essentially, I followed my mentor to Tennessee Tech. It was interesting to learn that you and Mr. Bob used to stay at the Holiday Inn in Cookeville.

Sounds like you are having fun working in your yard. You always liked to pamper your plants. I had no idea that you met my grandparents. My grandfather was the hub of our clan in Campground. He was highly respected by all. His kindness and wisdom are the qualities I most admired.

I would agree with you that my mother is lot more relaxed. Since my father's death, she has kept herself extremely busy—visiting friends, visiting the senior citizens center, and being involved in church work. She fishes and reads a lot, too. We visit her two or three times a year. In fact, our daughters spent two weeks with her this past summer. She enjoyed them very much. She plans to take a bus trip to visit us next summer.

I would like to let you in on something. Ms. Joan Thursh, articles editor of *Good Housekeeping*, informed me that the magazine plans to publish an article I submitted. It focuses on Gloria's triumphant effort to obtain the doctorate degree from Vanderbilt University in the face of obstacles—commuting 164 miles round-trip from Cookeville to Nashville and managing family responsibilities. Ms. Thursh could not give me a definite month for the release of the McGee article. Their decision is contingent upon when Phyllis George, wife of the Governor of Kentucky, gives birth to her child. The magazine plans to do a story about the First Family, especially the newborn... I shall keep you informed.

I am delighted that you are enjoying retirement in Heber Springs.

Most cordially,
Leo McGee
Assistant Dean, Extended Services

Aug. 21, 1984

Dear Leo & Gloria,

   I saw this about Shorter Jr. College and tho't Leo might like to see it, too. Hope they succeed in building up the school again.

   I really enjoyed seeing you two last May. That Leo really caught himself a beauty with a brain. I hope I get to see the article on your family in *Good Housekeeping*. Since I don't know when it is, please run off a copy on a machine and send it to me to gloat over. I'm so proud of your family. Willie B. has always been so special to me—a real friend. I called right away to tell her I saw you—first call no answer. She laughed later—"out fishing."

   Howard and I leave in about three weeks for Europe. We'll be there about five weeks then come home "luxuriantly" (in tourist class) on Queen E. II. I decided to blow some money I inherited on some real memories. I believe I told you we'd visit, among others, the A.F.S. student Bob and I kept from Germany. Rudigu—about 41/2 is near Neuenburg.

   I am mighty excited and preparing by a countdown schedule not unlike the astronauts—with house, yard, dog, etc. to arrange on top of packing, it takes time.

   Again—so good to meet Gloria and see Leo once more.

Love—
Mary Youngchild

Tennessee Technological University
Cookeville, Tennessee

August 27, 1984

Mrs. Mary Conner Youngchild
Wilburn Route 313
Heber Springs, AR 72543

Dear Mrs. Youngchild:

Thanks so very much for sending the Shorter Jr. College article. I am confident of the institution's survival. There have been ups and downs throughout its storied history. Fortunately, it always seems to land on level ground.

The institution means a great deal to my family. Three of us received degrees there. Moreover, many students from T.W. Daniel are graduates.

Please know that your visit to Cookeville meant a great deal to me! It was a delight for my wife, Gloria, to meet you. She is very familiar with my story about the impact you had on my life at an early age.

My mother frequently speaks of you. Indeed, she loves fishing. It is one of her favorite pastimes. She really loves being associated with the Senior Citizens Center, too. Friendships and activities are inspirational.

Do enjoy your trip to Europe. I vaguely remember my mother mentioning the exchange student, Rudigu.

I recently learned that the *Good Housekeeping* article about the McGee family is going to be in the October issue. Waiting with great anticipation!

Also, *Good Housekeeping*: "A Better Way" is in its second year of production. "The program presents up-beat personal profiles of women in all fields including movies, publishing, academics, politics, and business. Guests invited to appear on the show have included Geraldine Ferraro, Shirley Temple Black, Joanne Woodward, Heloise, and Phyllis Diller." King Features Entertainment of New York will come to Cookeville and spend three days filming Gloria at work and at home with her family. The McGee filming will immediately follow filming of Hillary Rodham Clinton in Little Rock. Gloria will fly to New York for the studio portion of the profile. The company invited me, too.

The half-hour program will run on LIFETIME Cable Network, February 21, 1985, at 1 pm (CST). Host, John Mack Carter, Editor-In-Chief of Good Housekeeping. Hillary Rodham Clinton will be on February 11 at 2 PM (CST).

My family is almost too excited to function properly. Cassandra sees this as an excellent laboratory experience for her since she is majoring in Broadcasting at UT.

I shall keep you posted.

Most cordially,
Leo McGee
Assistant Dean, Extended Services

December 10, 1985

Leo and Gloria—

Howard's arthritis and orthoscopic knee surgery have slowed him down considerably. Doctors' visits to Little Rock have become rather routine. Thankfully, there are many medical specialists within reach of Heber Springs. God knows, us old folks couldn't survive very long without them!

Couldn't wait to get my hands on *Good Housekeeping*! Found it in a local grocery. What a wonderful story you wrote, Leo. Howard loved it, too. Shared it all around. Had a group at my home to see the documentary about Gloria. How great that was—I'm so proud of you and your wife's accomplishments. It makes me so happy to know that you are such a supportive husband and such a good man. When you were a young man, I saw many of B's qualities in you—I just think the world of your mother. I think you know that—

. Saw the Hillary Clinton piece too. What an elegant Lady! Just what the State needs. Glad you alerted me—

So good to meet Jennifer on my second visit to Cookeville— and to see her folks. I always did have good taste in "yard help." My current "yard help" is me—and at age sixty-five—it's a bit wearing.

I haven't written B, but I'll do it soon—actually next—since I'm alphabetical. I'm so proud of you, Leo, but my pride can't touch your mother's. She is a remarkable Lady.

Love to the three I know and my best to the junior.
Mary Y.

Tennessee Technological University
Cookeville, Tennessee

January 6, 1986

Mrs. Mary Conner Youngchild
Wilburn Route 313
Heber Springs, AR 72543

Dear Mrs. Youngchild:

Enclosed is a newspaper article announcing my promotion at TTU. My new title is Assistant Vice President for Academic Affairs. I have many new responsibilities. I am very much looking forward to the new challenge, however. Gloria and I are enjoying our work at the University. She is an Assistant Professor of Early Childhood Education.

Cassandra is doing extremely well at the University of Tennessee. Jennifer is a freshman at the high school and is on the cheerleading squad. She loves it. She keeps her parents hopping—cheer practice, cheerleading camps, and ball games. She also takes tennis and piano lessons. At an earlier age, she was a top competitor in swimming (free style) and gymnastics. She received an invitation to become a member of the more advanced swimming program in Oak Ridge, Tennessee. Gloria and I were too busy in our jobs to accommodate. She has exceptional athletic ability, I am proud to say. I was definitely incapable of exhibiting that level of athleticism during my youth.

We had a wonderful visit with my mother during Christmas. The senior citizens center is a vital part of her life now. She seems very happy. Her positive attitude is so heartwarming. I am delighted.

Most cordially,
Leo McGee
Assistant Vice President for Academic Affairs

Greetings to Jennifer—the ice-cream eater

Mary & Howard Youngchild
Wilburn Route 313
Heber Springs, Ark. 72543

Jan. 31, 1986

Dear Leo and Gloria—

I was so delighted to get the notice of your expanded duties at Tenn. Tech. Your new title is imposing. I know it was a happy moment in the McGee household.

I have taken the liberty of forwarding it with a letter to the *News Observer* in Crossett. I also mentioned your *Good Housekeeping* article about Gloria's achievements. I hope you do not object.

I wrote B. a week ago—sent the article from G.H. I was having to thin out here. We have your family photo on the large bulletin board in our bedroom. (Not so exclusive there—Mary.)

Howard continues to improve—so much better than a year ago. He is in charge of the wood stove we use to supplement the furnace, and after a winter of doing it alone, I'm delighted. I stayed a bit scorched last year.

I'm so proud of you and so glad your talents are appreciated.

Sincerely,
Mary Youngchild

Sunday
Feb. 2, 1986

Dear Leo—

The University beat me to it! I was so delighted to find this nice article in this week's paper. I also enclosed an article about another Crossett graduate. Crossett did (and I guess still does) put emphasis on quality education.

Wanted to get this in the mail—
Sincerely,
Mary Y.

Tennessee Technological University
Cookeville, Tennessee

February 11, 1986

Mrs. Mary Conner Youngchild
Wilburn Route 313
Heber Springs, AR 72543

Dear Mrs. Youngchild:

It was exceptionally thoughtful and caring of you to share the piece about my promotion with the *News Observer*. The University has a very aggressive news services operation.

Your caring attitude toward my mother and now toward my immediate family is very precious. I am so delighted that our paths crossed. You continue to be an inspiration, enabling me to become more appreciative of the human spirit—catalyst, enabler, lasting friend. The world needs more people the likes of Mrs. Mary Conner Youngchild.

Thanks so very much for your continued support and friendship.

Most cordially,
Leo McGee
Assistant Vice President for Academic Affairs

December 10, 1986

Dear Leo and Gloria—

   Read in the *Observer* that Gloria had a promotion. The McGees have been all over the paper in the past year. Happy for you.

   I called Willie B. when we were in Crossett. We were about to leave since the water was gone—There had been some malfunction which caused a leak in Lucas Pond. It happened during the Rodeo—Leo—so you can imagine the consequences.

   Willie B. sounded good. She stays active, and that's good.

   I hope 1987 continues to bless your family.

With love,
Mary Youngchild

From the Desk of
Howard Youngchild

December 30, 1986

Dear Leo and Gloria—

    Tho't you'd like this write-up of your family reunion. Nice letter from Willie B.—glad her Christmas happy—

In haste—
Mary Youngchild

Tennessee Technological University
Cookeville, Tennessee

August 6, 1987

Mrs. Mary Conner Youngchild
Wilburn Route 313
Heber Springs, AR 72543

Dear Mrs. Youngchild:

Our eldest daughter, Cassandra, graduated with honors from the University of Tennessee in May with a degree in Broadcasting. She is a Video Journalist and an Associate Producer at CNN Headline News in Atlanta. Jennifer is still cheering and playing tennis—no more piano and competitive swimming. Gloria and I are still "doing what we do" at Tennessee Tech.

On occasions, I reflect on the days we spent clearing that thicketed lot for your new home. Truthfully, I was always afraid that I was going to step on a copperhead or disturb a nest of yellow jackets, bumblebees, or wasps. I knew there had to be plenty of ticks and chiggers out there. I confess that most of the time I was afraid. I often wondered why you did not seem the least bit bothered.

In spite of my fear, that was a very meaningful time in my life. Very powerful. I am most appreciative of the way you treated me. You made me feel special. Those kind gestures helped a great deal in molding me into who I am.

My mother was so happy when your family finally moved into the new home. She loved every inch of it. Your friendship with the squirrels was most intriguing to her. Your new house dominated my mother's conversations for months.

Most cordially,
Leo McGee
Assistant Vice President for Academic Affairs

January 21, 1988

Dear Leo,

It was hard for me to visualize a house going up on that lot covered with vines and briers. We cleared it—just the two of us. It took us weeks! I was so proud of us.

Remember how I used to bring our lunch to the lot, and the two of us would sit together and eat our meal. I still cherish those days—years. We were a great team. You and me—I was very proud when we completed the clearing job. Those years were great—I now look back on them with great pride and happiness.

I was so happy to get the clippings with the Christmas card from your family. I remember your grandfather well. I did not meet him at the time your mother was helping me, but later, one day in Safeway when he and your grandmother were there shopping with Willie B. She introduced us, and we shook hands warmly. It was then that I realized that the years that he had spent working had cost him some of his fingers. Since my granddad had missed part of a finger, that was nothing new to me. What I really appreciated was the fact that he was so willing to meet me and that there was no reticence over the missing digits. He was a proud, fine man, and the visit then with him as well as other times we met in Safeway, made me realize where your mother had inherited her strong character. I did not feel that I knew your grandmother as well, but she seemed to be a very nice lady. Most of my conversation was with that very outgoing grandfather of yours. I am so glad that you have given him the credit that he surely was due. I always see him there as I recall our meeting—very exuberant and proud. He gave you a fine foundation on which you have built.

We get CNN on the satellite, so I shall expect to see Cassandra someday. How wonderful that she graduated with honors at the U of Tenn. I think of Jennifer as the young girl for whom we ordered ice cream, but it won't be too long before she is college age. She has quite a record to live up "to." I certainly dangled that participle.

Did I tell you Willie B. sent us a yarn cat that she had made at the center? I am so proud to have it. She added that when she was younger, she didn't have time to make things like that, but had learned in her old age. I am so glad that she is able to do things she enjoys now. The good Lord knows that she worked hard raising her family and doing such a good job of it. I admire her so much. I have tried to suggest that she call me Mary since we are such old friends... and close in age tho' she leads me a few. I have made no progress on that.

I do all my housework now, but not as often as I once had it done. With a three hundred foot frontage, I do all the yard work but the mowing. It keeps me active, and I am sure I am healthier for it. I always did a lot of the heavier scrubbing and waxing in Crossett when I would get fired up, but B. kept us cleaned on a daily basis and ironed! If the Lord wants to punish me someday for my sins, fire wouldn't bother me nearly as much as constant dusting, ironing, and weeding. I don't mind the heavy "stuff" that shows when done and stays done a while.

I see that you continue to move up in the college, and I know that you do a good job helping young people to undertake reaching their goals. Your life is a great example. I actually had no idea there was enough cotton out where you used to live to pick, but there must have been more farm land between there and Hamburg to keep many a family busy. Bless that dear grandfather for what he taught you.

I actually learned more from my father's mother and my parents. My only living grandfather was up in the Northern part (UP) of Michigan and I wasn't around him enough to pick up much...except for a spanking I got for something my cousin had done.

With best wishes to you, Gloria, and Jennifer,
Mary Youngchild

Got article copied to send to the children, Deb and Robin.

Tennessee Technological University
Cookeville, Tennessee

March 9, 1988

Mrs. Mary Conner Youngchild
Wilburn Route 313
Heber Springs, AR 72543

Dear Mrs. Youngchild:

My boss has taken a position at the University of Tulsa. I am now Interim Vice President for Academic Affairs—number two administrator at the University. Obviously, there are many new challenges for me. My calmness surprises me. Wish me luck. I will need it—by the minute.

You are exactly right about my grandfather. He was very outgoing, warm, and friendly. He and my grandmother were a wonderful couple—good balance in personalities. As a kid, I loved being in their midst.

Delighted that you liked the yarn cat my mother sent. During my youth, she and other women in our area made quilts—lots of them. Gloria and I cherish the two she gave us as Christmas gifts. Our girls will have them to connect to their family heritage during later years.

Oh, there was cotton! Plenty of it in Ashley County! I have the physical and mental scars to show for it. I am so glad that you rescued my mother and me. I shall be forever thankful.

Again, wish me the best of luck in my new assignment.

Most cordially,
Leo McGee
Interim Vice President for Academic Affairs

From the Desk of
Howard Youngchild

July 6, 1988

Dear Leo—

I hope you and the family were at your family reunion. The way you felt about your granddad, I felt you were. This article was sent to me with the photo of Rudigu Hoffmann who was our German exchange student in 62/3. He was back in Crossett for his 25th high school reunion.

I picked him up on June 19. Called B., but she was at church. Later we called Willie B. so he could visit with her. Sorry we were in Crossett so briefly after his reunion.

She told me about your family reunion, and she was so happy and proud. I hope it was a whale of a success!

Arthritis plagues Howard, and now my sciatic nerve is giving me fits when I drive. I'm about to start therapy. I'm 68, but my folks live into their 90s, so I do hope and pray it helps.

We bought a 26' party barge now in our dockage. We should have done it 10 years ago.

My best to Gloria and Jennifer.

Best greetings—
Mary Youngchild

Rudigu a physicist and his wife an MD. She was not here this trip—was in '79.

Tennessee Technological University
Cookeville, Tennessee

August 9, 1988

Mrs. Mary Conner Youngchild
Wilburn Route 313
Heber Springs, AR 72543

Dear Mrs. Youngchild:

Indeed, my family did attend our family reunion in Crossett—Lake Georgia Pacific (Saturday), Campground AME Church (Sunday). So happy to see my mother and the rest of the family. My mother was in high heaven—seeing her large brood together once again. How delightful!

A 26' party barge! What a treat! Delighted that you are having lots of fun with it!

Most cordially,
Leo McGee
Interim Vice President for Academic Affairs

From the Desk of
Howard Youngchild

Nov. 12, 1988

Dear Leo—

Clipped this out a couple of weeks ago. I thought you might want to read about your old school—Philander Smith.

Howard had a new "knee" put in Oct. 13, and we've been home two plus weeks. Busy as a one-armed paperhanger tending to him for he is not able to be up taking care of himself wholly.

With the house, and a big yard full of leaves—and some transplanting, I don't even have time to fish.

Is Cassandra in broadcasting? I think of her when CNN comes on.

Best of all to you all—
Mary Y.

Tennessee Technological University
Cookeville, Tennessee

November 22, 1988

Mrs. Mary Conner Youngchild
Wilburn Route 313
Heber Springs, AR 72543

Dear Mrs. Youngchild:

Thanks for sending the article about Philander Smith. Excellent editorial. Dr. Titus seems to be an outstanding president.

I have many fond memories of the institution. More importantly, I found Gloria there! I nearly lost the chance to hold on to her in 1962 when the Draft Board in Hamburg threatened to send MPs to campus to pick me up because I did not check in at age 18. Your husband, Mr. Bob, came to my rescue! I shall be forever thankful. I can still hear his calm, collected, and soothing voice about the matter as if it were yesterday.

"Leo," he said, "don't pay any attention to that letter. Don't even respond to it. I'll take care of it. Go on about your business at the college. You know Mary and I think the world of you. We'll always help you in any way we can. Remember, all you have to do is ask."

I never heard another word from the Draft Board. What a relief! What a heavy burden off my mind! I doubt that you remember any of this. However, the evening I called for Mr. Bob, you answered the phone. I was really nervous and scared out of my wits. The uncertainty nearly killed me. Mr. Bob literally saved me from destruction—and from losing my dear Gloria!

Cassandra did major in Broadcasting but works behind the scenes at CNN Headline News—Video Journalist and Associate Producer.

Most cordially,
Leo McGee
Interim Vice President for Academic Affairs

Trout Haven
Wilburn Route 313
Heber Springs, Ark. 72543

September 29, 1990

Dear Leo and Gloria,

This is some of the stationery that we concocted in the flush of moving to Heber Springs from Crossett back in 1977. We only catch trout, but the fish I sketched bears no resemblance to one. I believe I was marked by the memory of South Arkansas catfish.

I was so pleased to get Leo's letter. I love to write letters, and there are so few people who will write. Thank you so much.

I was so pleased to read about the marvelous scholarship Jennifer was awarded. That should certainly help you two in her education. It was marvelous to know that she was one of four in the State to receive a scholarship...a real "plum." I loved the family picture, too, of Jennifer's homecoming reign. You are a good-looking family. Leo must have kept up that jogging to stay so slim.

Cassandra looks great. I would not be surprised to see her some day in a national TV assignment for NBC. You have so much to be proud of in the success of your children as well as yourselves.

I could not help but remember an occasion when Debby had just left the nest. Bob was mooning around about how much he missed her when she went to Hendrix for the freshman year. I said I didn't miss her that much since her comings and goings were no longer under my supervision. If she came in late, I didn't have to worry. That took care of that.

Back to Bob and Debby... I told him that if she were still living at home, she wouldn't be there in the early evening. He answered that he knew that, but she would be returning later. I came back with the fact that when she did and woke him up, he would yell at her. His retort was that she would know that he loved her anyway. I have chuckled over that for years.

Howard had a minor stroke called TIA caused by a high "sed rate" in his blood. He was fine by morning after his attack. However, he was taken to Little Rock by ambulance for fear it could be a true stroke and his vascular system and heart were checked thoroughly. He had no problems there. So, he is on Prednisone which has made him gain, but he needed the weight. We were able to reduce the dosage this week and may be able to again in two weeks. I hope so. The steroids are dangerous as well as helpful.

I am fine except for a very bad curvature of my back, which has caused problems with my sacroiliac in my old age. I can work hard in the yard, but let me step out of the car wrong, sit at an angle, or such, and I hurt like the dickens. I try to be good, move slowly, take my time, sit straight, etc., but it's not my nature to move slowly. I am having problems learning.

It's been a long hot summer, and the weeds grew madly during the 100 degree weather when I declined to weed. I am catching up now that fall has come, and the weather moderated somewhat.

I have no recent news of Willie B., but I feel she will be going on for years. She is a dear lady!

Thanks for the pictures...put the family on my picture board in the bedroom. That way I can keep up better than in books.

Best of all,
Mary Youngchild

Sept. 30, 1990

Dear Leo—

Mailed your letter yesterday and saw this today. I suppose he is a cousin—or at least related.

Sorted photos today and found these prints of Willie B. and me made in 1989. Good-looking gals! We are such a pair and good friends!

Best of all—
M. Y.

Tennessee Technological University
Cookeville, Tennessee

November 26, 1990

Mrs. Mary Youngchild
Wilburn Route 313
Heber Springs, AR 72543

Dear Mrs. Youngchild:

Thanks for sending the clipping from the *Arkansas Gazette*. Indeed, Thomas Lowe Jr. is a cousin. I believe he is a year behind Jennifer. I see that "he has been named as a semi-finalist in the National Achievement Program for Outstanding Black Students." What an accomplishment! I understand that he wants to study engineering at Louisiana Tech.

Jennifer is a freshman at the University of Tennessee. She was ONE popular student at Cookeville High. In addition to being captain of the cheerleading squad, she was Homecoming Queen and voted Miss Cookeville High. She hopes to make the cheerleading squad at UT.

Thanks for the compliment about my weight. I do run some, but my football knees remind me that running is perhaps not a good idea. I have taken tennis lessons and plan to put that to use.

Now that Cassandra is on the air—a reporter at WBIR-TV, NBC affiliate, Knoxville—I am sure she would be delighted about your premonition of national exposure.

We will visit my mother during the Christmas holidays. I am yearning for that loving embrace.

Most cordially,
Leo McGee
Associate Vice President for Academic Affairs

December 4, 1990

Dear Leo and Gloria,

Our yard continues to be my joy. I have replaced vegetables with blossoms…a few tomatoes, peppers, and eggplants are tucked in among the blossoms. I am endeavoring to grow perennials realizing that time will make it difficult to work as hard as I now do. My macro-photographs of flowers and butterflies along with pictures of the river, mountains, and sunsets help keep my creative soul satisfied.

I love sending lengthy letters despite Ann Landers. I only wish people I write would let me know how they and theirs are doing. Leo. I am so glad that you keep me up with the girls and yourselves.

Luther Wimberly died recently Leo. I don't know if you remember him, but his wife Bessie Mae is a good friend of your mother and I. I believe she has Alzheimer's (SP) so it will be easier for her now. That is such a terribly debilitating disease. I wrote and had a short note from your mother.

I hope that the girls are able to be with you this holiday season.

With love,
M.

Tennessee Technological University
Cookeville, Tennessee

January 24, 1991

Mrs. Mary Youngchild
Wilburn Route 313
Heber Springs, AR 72543

Dear Mrs. Youngchild:

Mr. Luther "Bubba" Wimberly was somewhat of a revered cousin. He was kind to everybody, gentle, principled, and loved by all—my mother's first cousin. His mother and my grandfather were siblings. His wife, Mrs. Bessie Mae, is a wonderful person as well. It hurts me deeply to hear about her illness.

You and I definitely have something in common—love of yard work. I picked up that habit from you. I will pick yard work over ANY chore that Gloria can concoct. I absolutely love mowing, edging, and trimming. No weeding and no vegetable gardening, however... I even have an excellent collection of hydrangeas. You introduced me to the hydrangea plant. I was not at all fond of it back then. It seemed as if I could never quench their thirst—blooms drooped and foliage wilted in that hot summer heat in Crossett. Now, Gloria and I just love our collection. Blooms everywhere!

Jennifer is in her second semester at UT. She seems to be very happy and focused.

Most cordially,
Leo McGee
Associate Vice President for Academic Affairs

May 22, 1991

Dear Leo,

I saw this in the *Gazette* the other day…wondered if it wasn't a relative of yours. Whether or not, it is great to receive that marvelous scholarship, and I am proud for him. College costs so much now that few families can do it without help. I don't need to tell you about the business you are in!

I went in April to the 50th Anniversary of the class of 1941 at Hendrix. I started with the group, but I dropped out with an AA degree to go to Crossett after I married Bob Conner who had finished six years at the U of Cincinnati the year before I got out of high school. He was ready to settle down, and fortunately I never had to work. A young woman now days needs to have a way to make a living because the stay-home wife is almost a thing of the past.

It was great fun to see all my old friends…and I do mean old… and to have a ribbon with a large medal hung around my neck. Howard celebrated his 79th birthday wearing a badge that declared that he was married to Mary Meek. I tho't that was pretty sporting.

I was so happy when Willie B. wrote me after I sent the birthday card, and she enclosed a lovely card for a good friend. She finally addressed me as Mary…and I was so happy. We are friends…and she is older than I.

I am 72 now. My health is excellent. I take an arthritis pill, but most people my age do. I keep up a huge yard…all but mowing…300 feet across the front. My flowers are lovely, and tho' there is a great deal of work, I am happy doing it.

You may already have this clipping, but I tho't I would send it just in case.

Hope all three of your girls are fine.

Love—
Mary Y.

Tennessee Technological University
Cookeville, Tennessee

May 27, 1991

Mrs. Mary Youngchild
Wilburn Route 313
Heber Springs, AR 72543

Dear Mrs. Youngchild:

It was so good to hear from you. Thanks for sending the article from the *Gazette*. Yes, Thomas Lowe Jr. is a cousin. The $8,000 Georgia Pacific Scholarship he received is most impressive! We are all proud of his accomplishments. These funds will serve him well at Louisiana Tech.

My mother cherishes the relationship that you all have. She has thought the world of you since the day you all met. Ditto for me. You have always been a kind, caring, and gentle person. It has truly been a pleasure and a blessing knowing you all these years. Thank you for caring.

Our youngest daughter, Jennifer, completed her first year at the University of Tennessee with academic honors. She also made the cheerleader squad! She is thrilled. So are her parents and sister. The eldest, Cassandra, is still a reporter for the NBC affiliate in Knoxville.

My wife, Gloria, and I are enjoying an empty nest. We are both heavily involved in our work at the University.

Hope to see you at some point in the future.

Most cordially,
Leo McGee
Associate Vice President for Academic Affairs

December 10, 1991

Dear Leo and Gloria,

Unbelievable as it seems, Howard and I celebrated our 15th anniversary in October with our 16th Christmas together coming soon.

Since health always seems to be the opening topic, I will say that Howard continues to have problems with arthritis which ably predicts weather changes. At the moment, he is pretty stove up making trips out of here rather rare. Going for a haircut one day, he remarked that he was like a cat…he had nine lives! He had successful cataract surgery done here by a delightful young lady ophthalmologist who spoiled him outrageously. He is happy to be able to read more easily with colors much brighter.

I am rocking along with few problems. A bit of arthritis and a lower back that bi-monthly trips to the chiropractor keeps happy. My shrinking two plus inches has put pressure on my curvature.

We can take no fascinating vacations because home is where Howard feels best. He was a good sport in April celebrating his 79th birthday at Hendrix College with me when we joined my classmates for a 50th Graduation Reunion.

We are enjoying the arrival of the winter bird, which Howard feeds profusely. The yard and the flowerbeds are still my love…way too much for me to do, but how else to stay "young" and agile. I have three beds of annuals and perennials 45' by 8', which keeps me weeding frequently. The daffodils and crocus followed by the wild flower garden in the early spring are a very special joy and macro-lens camera target.

Wishing you a joyous season and happy 1992!

Mary Y.

March 11, 1992

Dear Leo and Gloria,

I was delighted to receive the article about your family's years in Cookeville. I sent it on to Debby who also tho't it was excellent.

As far as I am concerned, as you know, Cookeville is the better for the arrival of you four.

Spring came early as you know, and I'm way ahead of my yard schedule. I may be almost 73—but I can put out a great day's work in the yard. It's almost a tonic for me—and I am sure a reason I am as healthy as I am. I'm developing a new area in our 300' front yard about 200' deep. I do all but the mowing.

This photo is along the walk to the front porch—my version of an English garden where it does get hot.

Best to you—
Mary Y.

Tennessee Technological University
Cookeville, Tennessee

April 9, 1992

Mrs. Mary Youngchild
Wilburn Route 313
Heber Springs, AR 72543

Dear Mrs. Youngchild:

When I left Little Rock in 1964 for Chicago, I expected to be in a major city for the rest of my life. While living in Nashville, Gloria and I came to Cookeville to consider positions at Tennessee Tech in 1977. After our visit, I thought Cookeville was perfect for the family. Gloria and Cassandra, not so much. At age 4, it did not matter to Jennifer.

Many years later, both Gloria and I think the move was a very positive one for the entire family. All of us seemed to have made giant strides here. Cookeville is a very welcoming community. What a delight for us! Sharing our story seemed most appropriate. Glad you liked it.

We are looking forward to visiting my mother soon. We talk regularly by phone. You always drift into our conversations.

Most cordially,
Leo McGee
Associate Vice President for Academic Affairs

December 10, 1992

Dear Leo and Gloria,

I hadn't been to Crossett since June '91 and hear very little about it. After so many years there, it does feel strange. Have to admit I like the country here better—rolling hills, some "small" mountains, and my lovely river just below the bank.

I hope Willie B. is doing all right. She has some health problems that cause concern. She is a strong woman with a good attitude—and that helps. You know how I've always admired her.

Jennifer must be in her second year—or is it third year of college. The older I get—the faster time flies.

My love and holiday wishes,
Mary

Tennessee Technological University
Cookeville, Tennessee

January 20, 1993

Mrs. Mary Youngchild
Wilburn Route 313
Heber Springs, AR 72543

Dear Mrs. Youngchild:

We visited my mother during the holidays. Her health is not what it used to be. As usual, she is taking things in stride. Absolutely no complaining about her declining health. I loved seeing her and spending time there. Gloria and I helped in the kitchen—mostly Gloria.

Jennifer is in her third year at UT and enjoying every aspect of college life. She is as full of energy as ever—cheering away for the Volunteers!

Most cordially,
Leo McGee
Associate Vice President for Academic Affairs

December 14, 1993

Dear Leo and Gloria—

I watched Tenn/Ark on TV and wondered if Jennifer were a cheerleader that day. Have to admit I cannot sit thru a game, but wander in and out past the TV.

It's been a wild spring and summer. I was in Crossett in May and chatted on the phone with Willie B—So many folks and so little time.

Willie B. never got my letter last Christmas—I wrote on her birthday and asked. Rudigu, the exchange student, now 49, in Germany didn't either. Always wonder where they go! Incidentally, Rudigu's daughter Sandra age 16 is an AFS student in Irvine, California. On edge of fires—but safe.

Hope all you folks are well and prospering. We're homebound pretty much—have to watch Howard for fluid build-up on his heart. We'll never see Alaska, but I let him dream.

Love to all—
Mary

From the Desk of
Howard Youngchild

Jan. 26, 1994

Dear McGees—

I loved that picture of Jennifer—legs pointing East and West way up in the air. I tho't I'd get a chance to see her when Tennessee played NY's Day—The first shot of the cheerleaders early in the introduction found me still in the kitchen peeking thru the pass thru. Too far away. So—I went and sat in front of the TV to be sure I would see them. I had a glimpse now and then—but no Jennifer—no complete group.

Finally I was forced to make a potty trip—Howard yelled—"Here they are"—but I missed them. Later I had to leave again and H. swears he saw them all. I enjoyed the game and sat longer than I have for any game this season. I am sorry I missed her.

My usual method of watching football is to continue some odd job and watch as I pass the TV. The old Presbyterian (Scotch) work ethic is too ingrained in me to relax and sit when there is something that needs to be done. Believe me—with all I have to do here with Howard sick keeps me plenty busy.

Called B. Saturday & she wasn't home. Will try again. I wrote her on her birthday. Hard to believe she's 84—and that I will hit 74 soon.

Tell Jennifer I tried—and I yelled for the Vols.

Happy 1994
Mary Y.

Tennessee Technological University
Cookeville, Tennessee

February 7, 1994

Mrs. Mary Youngchild
Wilburn Route 313
Heber Springs, AR 72543

Dear Mrs. Youngchild:

It was good to hear from you. Sorry you missed Jennifer. She is simply having a ball at UT. We are thrilled that she is doing well academically. Her grade point average is well over 3.0 on a 4.0 scale.

Gloria and I are doing fine. She is an Associate Professor of Education. She teaches courses in Early Childhood Education. I am an Associate Vice President for Academic Affairs, which means that my administrative unit is over all the various colleges on campus—Agriculture and Home Economics, Arts and Sciences, Business Administration, Education, Engineering, and Nursing.

I visited my mother on two sad occasions during the fall. One of my sisters and her husband passed away within six weeks of each other. We will miss them terribly as they were the hub of a large clan.

Dr. Larry Miller is no longer at Tennessee Tech. He now lives in Kansas.

Most cordially,
Leo McGee
Associate Vice President for Academic Affairs

December 6, 1994

Dear Leo and Gloria,

So good to see Willie B—and to see her getting around so well on her prosthesis. I always have been amazed at her ability to adjust. She's quite a "gal." We met at the senior citizens center for a good visit. I didn't know about the leg until I called her in Crossett to make arrangements.

Saw the hydrangeas you moved for me way back in 1959—they lived and thrived. We were pretty good gardeners. Enjoyed a walk through my old yard.

I am still endeavoring to catch glimpses of Jenny on TV during U of T football games. Howard loves Peyton Manning—he says, as he did his father, Archie, when he played at Ole Miss.

Best to all the McGees,
Mary

Tennessee Technological University
Cookeville, Tennessee

January 20, 1995

Mrs. Mary Youngchild
Wilburn Route 313
Heber Springs, AR 72543

Dear Mrs. Youngchild:

My mother's bout with that "devilish diabetes" progressed rather precipitously. "Devilish diabetes" is what she calls it. First, it was the amputation of a section of a toe, then the entire toe, then the leg just below the knee.

It was amazing how calm she was throughout the ordeal. After the doctor had experimented with removing a section of the toe and then the entire toe, my mother actually scolded the doctor a bit. "Doctor," she said, "if you have to take the leg off, just go on and do it and stop fooling around. I want to hurry up and get back home."

Although this situation was most stressful for me, I could not help but chuckle a bit. I doubt that many people in the universe would have an upbeat spirit in such a trying time. It was obviously not that trying for my mother. She is amazing!

In addition to that, she learned to walk with her prosthesis rather easily. She still drives. Occasionally, she chauffeurs her friends to appointments and such.

We grew even closer during the two weeks I spent taking care of her. It was a pleasure to be her caretaker. We talk a lot—more than ever before. I loved learning more about our family history... She wanted me to let you know that she is doing fine. I assured her I would.

Jennifer is in her last year of cheerleading. Gloria and I will truly miss going to Knoxville to watch her cheer in person as well as on TV.

I clearly remember moving those hydrangeas in your yard. It took all day one Saturday because the ground was so dry and hard. I am delighted that they are thriving. Yes, we were indeed "pretty good" gardeners. That experience of transplanting those hydrangeas has given me great confidence in transplanting shrubs in my own yard—a very valuable learning experience. No doubt, you would be pleased with the incremental expansion of the McGee Hydrangea Garden.

Most cordially,
Leo McGee
Associate Vice President for Academic Affairs

Dec. 14, 1995

Dear Leo and Gloria,

Howard has his usual problems with arthritis and breathing, but I stole the spotlight by being hauled to Little Rock in an ambulance with congestive heart failure on October18. I had been painting the large deck for three weeks during which I attributed an expanding waist to a spastic colon, took pills for the same, and did my thing until the afternoon I couldn't draw a breath. I am never really sick so it was a shock to me, to Howard, and to our friends… "Mary is never sick!"

When Willie B called me while I was recuperating, she told me you all were concerned because you had not heard from me. It was so good to hear her voice and know that you were thinking of me. I did watch the Tennessee ball game over the New Years—Crocodile Bowl, I think—and I am sure that this time I finally saw Jennifer. There was a real close-up as she passed the camera as well as several shots of the group. I cannot remember at this moment where she is now but I do recall you all are going to be grandparents via Cassandra. Congratulations! I recall that Jenny is continuing her education…doctor? What?

My sister, Tweetie, stayed with me after my hospitalization. I have to admit I don't mind giving up the vacuuming, but I sure do hate to give up the yard work…the harder, the messier, the happier I was!

I had planned to go to Crossett to visit Robin and down to see Debby in Lafayette, LA, about the time I ended up in the hospital. I am grateful that my heart is responding to the care. I have given up salt, the hard work, and a few other things. However, I have never been bored so I am sure that I will find plenty of things to do to fill my days. I may even get back to reading like I should.

I cannot believe that Willie B is about to be 86. She has given you good genes and a fine example, Leo. I don't need to tell you that! Her accepting the leg was an example for all of us!

Have a happy holiday season. I know you will be happy if the girls are close by.

Happy Holidays and Love—
Mary

Tennessee Technological University
Cookeville, Tennessee

December 20, 1995

Mrs. Mary Youngchild
Wilburn Route 313
Heber Springs, AR 72543

Dear Mrs. Youngchild:

Indeed, we are expecting our first grandchild. Grandchild! Can you believe it? Gee, how time does fly! I am too young to be a grandfather. My comrades would perhaps say I am only "young at heart," however. The kid who used to work in your yard is now 54 and has daughters age thirty and twenty-three. Cassandra, the eldest, is expecting. She is due in April. She is a co-anchor on the weekend for the NBC-TV affiliate in Knoxville.

Jennifer is a first-year medical student at East Tennessee State University and seems to be enjoying every minute of it. Her self-discipline scares her parents nearly to death. She has been that way all of her life. She spent the entire Thanksgiving break knee-deep in books. We are very proud of her accomplishments and look forward to having the first doctor in the McGee family. Medical doctor, that is. I was the first—Education.

Gloria and I are enjoying the empty nest syndrome and are rejoicing in the happiness of our daughters. We continue to enjoy our work at Tennessee Tech, where we have been for close to nineteen years. It is very likely that Gloria will get a professorial promotion this academic year—to full Professor of Education. I am a full Professor of Education and an Associate Vice President for Academic Affairs. I am enjoying my hobbies more than ever—tennis, creative writing, and hydrangea gardening. I am currently working on an autobiography. I hope to complete it during the spring of '96.

I was deeply saddened to hear about the problem you had with your heart but am delighted to know you are much better now. I wish you the absolute very best during your recovery. I have confidence that you will soon be back to normal.

My mother is an incredible woman. She has taken her problems with diabetes in stride. The average human would have trouble dealing with the loss of a portion of a leg, but not my mother. She remains in good spirits. She simply boggles my mind. I plan to visit with her for a spell after Christmas.

I wonder if you have a photograph of you and Mr. Bob together that you would be willing to share with me. I would love to have a visual of you two.

With very best wishes for the holiday season!

Most cordially,
Leo McGee
Associate Vice President for Academic Affairs

March 7, 1996

Dear Leo,

I received in the mail from Julia Alice Oaklief yesterday the two sections of the *Observer* that related to articles about people who had left Crossett, etc. I was so delighted and more so when I found the article about you and your family. My typewriter has a way of sneaking in extra letters. Pardon now for the entire letter.

I was pleased to read about the trip you and Bob took to see the effluent (SP) area known as Stink Creek. I probably may have known about it at the time, but forgot. At any rate, Bob was a dear man who loved his fellow man. It's been almost 21 years since I lost him, but I will always enjoy my memories. I chuckle to myself that I can lay beside Howard and find myself back in Crossett raising the kids with Bob in my dreams. In all fairness, Howard will probably be in the next dream. I have very vivid dreams many of which, after all these years, are still centered in Crossett.

I enjoyed the whole article, but a lot of it I already knew thanks to the fact that we keep in touch. I don't remember when the blessed event is due to occur. I hope you will let me know about the new arrival when he/she arrives.

I have been planning to send this photo over since Christmas. I really planned to copy it with my camera but never got it done. I will leave that up to you. I have discovered that I can make copies with the micro setting on my Fujica camera done outside on a sunny day before 10:00 o'clock and after 4:00 P.M. I have had very good luck. I told your mother when I wrote for her birthday that I was going to send it…sorry I was so pokey. This picture was done when we were leaving Crossett for the Philadelphia area in 1973. He was doing consulting for Scott Paper after Crossett Paper Mill gave him one of its famous Georgia Pacific surprises, demoting him without warning…or I might add…without reason. But this is past history. This was at a party just before we left in the summer of 1973. I am so happy that we had the two years in Philadelphia and Greenville, SC. Because we had such a happy time away from the mill and almost like honeymooners. I will always cherish the memory of Bob telling me as we drove across Tennessee on I40 that he was so glad that he had married me. That was about four weeks before his early death… I woke to find him dying in the bed beside me. It was apparently some form of heart attack, but since the children were adopted, there was no reason to have an autopsy. His own dad had a stroke at the same age and died within the year. Better for Bob to go than to be chained to a wheelchair as active as he was. Enough reminiscing.

Howard has had a terrible time with his arthritis this winter. He hurts so much. He also is having more need for oxygen than earlier. I expect our trips out of town to eat lunch are over.

I am doing quite a bit better. My heart medicine has been adjusted so that I feel much better. Too much had left me light-headed.

I am recovering from a strep throat at the moment. I caught it the day it began and started antibiotics, thank goodness. They do not want me to have any more illness which can worsen the heart. I certainly am trying to be more careful. I was pretty careless before with good health, I thought, and the love of hard work.

I am driving to El Dorado in two weeks to see my sister. We will leave the next day for Lafayette, LA, to spend a long weekend with Debby. A nurse's aide will stay here with Howard. He also has home health nurses coming in as well as a housekeeper weekly.

After the trip to Deb's, we will return to El Dorado and I will get to Crossett for some time before I come home. Looking forward to visiting Robin and his family.

Today is cold! The first flowers are going to get nipped tonight as the temps dip down into the single figures. I have been enjoying watching the early bulbs…some of which came from Pearl Ramseurs' old place…blooming, and the first of the early wild flowers opening. I love them.

As I approach my 77th birthday, I wonder at your very remarkable mother. I admire her so much as well as loving her for our time together when I went from my 30's to my 50's, as I recall. Willie B is one sharp lady and not a lazy bone in her body.

I didn't mean to take up the day writing a letter to tie you up so long.

When you are finished with the photo, you may return it. I trust you completely.

Let me know about the book signing, what and when.

My love to Gloria and the girls even tho' the latter are flown from the nest for the most part. How proud you must be of them, too.

Love,
Mary Youngchild

Tennessee Technological University
Cookeville, Tennessee

March 24, 1996

Mrs. Mary Youngchild
Wilburn 313
Heber Springs, AR 72543

Dear Mrs. Youngchild:

Thanks so very much for sending me the lovely photo of you and Mr. Bob. I had the Photo Department at the University to make copies for me. It brought back very pleasant memories.

Indeed, Mr. Bob was a fine human being. Exceptional! He was always very kind and gentle to me. I appreciated that very much. I shall never forget our trip to Stink Creek. I had no knowledge of its existence nor how valuable it was to the town of Crossett and the Paper Mill. What an eye-opening experience!

When I reflect on my years in Crossett, pleasant memories of my relationship with Mrs. and Mr. Conner always come into focus. The Conner family had an awful lot to do with my development and my view of human relations. The way you all treated me and my mother elevated our self-esteem tremendously. Also, assisted in molding me in a very special way. I considered our relationship back then and to this day to be very special and to some degree most unique.

We had two very big snows in Cookeville. The latest one was last week—on the first day of spring. My daffodils did not have much of a chance. I planted lots of them last fall and was looking forward with great anticipation to their beautiful yellow blooms, but to no avail. Thanks to the huge unexpected snow.

Jennifer spent two weeks with us this month. We were thrilled to have her home. One week was spring break and the other was to do an internship with a pediatrician in Cookeville. She is considering that specialty as a career option. She really enjoyed making the rounds at the hospital with the mentor doctor. He introduced her to his patients as his student doctor. The patients consistently referred to her as Dr. McGee. Jenny was completely overwhelmed but loved every minute of it.

While Jennifer was home, the three of us took a trip to Little Rock. Jenny and I tagged along with Gloria to one of her regional conferences. It was good to get by Philander Smith College and visit with old classmates and some faculty. Downtown was disappointing, however. Many stores on Main Street were boarded-up. Some major cities have found ways to upgrade downtown sections—not Little Rock, as of yet anyway. It is very sad. The architecture of many of the buildings is so magnificent.

Cassandra is expecting to deliver our grandchild in about four weeks. We are so excited. I cannot wait to install gymnastics apparatus in her backyard as I did for the girls when they were young. I gave them a real advantage in the cheerleading business.

It is true that I am attempting to write a memoir, but the real hurdle is to convince a publishing house to invest in it. That may or may not happen. I am certainly hoping that it does.

I talked with my mother yesterday. She seems to be holding her own quite well.

Again, thanks for sending the photo.

Most cordially,
Leo McGee
Associate Vice President for Academic Affairs

Wishing you all the joys
Of the Christmas Season

Have a wonderful Christmas

12-20-96

Mrs. Mary Youngchild,

Jordan Erica, our granddaughter, is seven months.

Jennifer is in her second year of medical school. She will likely choose General Surgery. She is a very determined young lady.

My mother is in good spirits as usual.

My memoir manuscript is at a publishing house in Little Rock.

Love,
Leo, Gloria, and Jenny

December 14, 1997

Dear Leo and Gloria,

I was so happy to catch a visit with Willie B at the senior center a couple of week ago. Debby and I had gone to Crossett the day after Thanksgiving…went to the center but it was closed. We called B. at home, but she was in Pine Bluff. She had wanted to see her, too. I went back next week, and my first stop was the center at noon. She was smiling toward the door, and I walked up and stood in front of her and she realized who was there. We had a good big hug and a great visit. It is so good that she is still so clear and active. We talk now and then on the phone since I get 8 hours on my cellular phone for $10 over the regular fee…nights and weekends. It is only in Arkansas… and helps with my calls to my sister and other good friends.

I love to visit Crossett but I am sure glad I don't live there. I haven't the fondest memories of Georgia Pacific and the downtown section has run down so much. There are lovely new housing areas… where all the people come from I don't know because they tell me the population remains about the same. It's all built up SE of Lucas Pond with fancy homes.

Howard's illness has not made my life easy, but with help (and I still need more), we can handle it at home. I don't get out much, but since my heart failure, I don't have quite as much drive as I did before.

Leo, those hydrangeas we moved to 1000 Willow Circle are still going strong after about 38 years. I went thru the house. The new owners love it so much that it didn't even make me unhappy. I told her how to take care of the hydrangeas and other plants, and she was tickled to death. They moved in last summer.

Anxious to hear how you two and the girls are doing.

Merry Christmas and Love,
Mary

January 5, 1998

Dear Mrs. Youngchild:

The McGee family had another blessed year. Jordan, our nearly two-year-old granddaughter, brought much joy to her grandparents.

Cassandra is still co-anchor on weekends for the NBC-TV affiliate in Knoxville. Jennifer is in her third year of medical school. We miss seeing her cheer during the UT football games.

Gloria and I are still enjoying our work at Tennessee Tech. We are into our 21st year. We will most likely conclude or careers here.

My mother never ceases to amaze me. She is always in such good spirits and continues to be very active in center activities. I am delighted that you got a chance to visit with her. She always enjoys that.

Best wishes in '98.

Love,
Leo and Gloria

Dec. 3 '98

Dear Leo and Gloria—

Robin and I went by the sr. center in Crossett in September—walked up and just stood in front of Willie B.—she focused and was as excited as we were.

We had a nice "remembering" visit while she ate. She amazes me with her clear mind and agility despite her prosthesis.

Howard has been gone 10 months. I have rested and relaxed because the stress of his illness—and a lot of our marriage (he loved beer—lots of beer) had worn me down. I do feel I look much better. I have become reacquainted with my kids and other family members. I seldom could get away. Thanksgiving was great in El Dorado at my sister's house. I hope to return Christmas if all goes well. I pray no heart failure.

Love to all—M.

January 7, 1999

Dear Mrs. Youngchild,

I always look forward to receiving your Christmas letter. I was saddened to learn that Mr. Youngchild passed away. May your grief continue to be replaced by pleasant memories of the past.

My mother seems to be in good spirits despite her health problems. Her two sisters passed away during the year. She is the only one left in her immediate family. She will soon be 89 but still drives and goes to the center daily. The center is her life now. She has lots of friends there and the activities keep her quite busy and alert. I am truly delighted that she has something in her life that she really enjoys. She seems to spend almost no time grieving about the condition of her health, which is most amazing. That is who she is.

After Jordan came along, Cassandra took a job with the Chamber of Commerce in Knoxville as Marketing Director. She left the co-anchor position with the NBC-TV affiliate.

Jennifer will graduate from medical school this spring. Currently, she is interviewing for a residency position for the fall. You perhaps have learned by now that her old football team, Tennessee, won the national championship.

Gloria and I are beginning to look a lot more like grandparents. We are into our twenty-second year at Tennessee Tech. We love it.

Best wishes during the year!

Love,
Leo and Gloria

March 1, 1999

Dear Leo—

Tho't you'd like to see this write up tho' I'm sure you are kept up thru the school.

Enjoyed your letter—you "old folks" at home alone while the girls move on. Can scarcely believe Jennifer—that young thing who came to Holiday Inn with you two to meet Howard and me and ate ice cream—could be so far along in her medical education. The older I get, the faster time flies.

My sister, Debby, and I leave for Amsterdam April 23—we fly KHM direct from Memphis. Will be met by German friends we met in Crossett when he was installing presses at the Flake Board Plant—Next we go to see Rudigu and Erica—you remember he was my exchange student 62/63. She is a doctor, so I'll be in good hands.

Deb goes home after two weeks, but Tweetie and I continue to Brussels, London, York, and Edinburgh. We have English, German, and Scotch ancestry—so want to check on where they came from—not specific places except in Germany.

We'll fly home May 17—I bet I sleep a week when we get back!

My black cat, Sultan, and I are doing well. I do not get lonesome—enjoy the quiet here at home.

Flowers out and I'm ready to do yard work as much as I'm allowed to do.

Nice letter from B. after her birthday. Must call her soon.

Best of all—and Love
M.

Warmest wishes
for a holiday
that's bright with all the delights
of the season.

12-14-99

Mrs. Youngchild,

Thanks for the article regarding Philander Smith College's president. Sounds as if he is the right person for the job.

Jennifer graduated from medical school and is now in residency at Tulane University in New Orleans. Cassandra chose to give up the anchor position and is now working with the Knoxville Chamber of Commerce in Public Relations.

Gloria and I are still enjoying our work. I saw my mother at a niece's wedding in Pine Bluff a few weeks ago.

Love,
Leo and Gloria

Dec. 6, '00

Dear Leo and Gloria—

This has been a great year for me. I turned 80 years old in April. I'm trying to emulate your mother, Leo, by living long and staying busy.

Our trip was wonderful—but when my sister and I were alone and having to handle our own luggage on and off trains that stop only briefly, we laughed at ourselves. She had to do the heavy ones and I the carry-ons.

After I recovered from the three and a half weeks, I decided to do as promised. Late one afternoon I called Gateway and ordered my first computer. I was no longer able to keep up in the family, and I decided at 80, I wanted a challenge to keep my mind sharp. It was installed the next week. Not having had typing and no preparation, I have worked hard and long. Accepting the fact you dive in and do things and occasionally get scolded by the computer, but you really cannot hurt it, helped me a lot. My sister, a Tennessee neighbor who spends time next door, and a beloved friend across the river have, with the help from others, held my hand. I love it!

The computer has opened my eyes to a new world of writing and fun. I do not do chat rooms—so far, not much research—but being able to do those things is a thrill!

Robin and Marcie are in Crossett. Deb continues in Lafayette. I stay involved with my church, play bridge weekly, and write on the computer

Sultan, my black cat, and I are content enjoying our home. He doesn't go out so cannot share my joy there tho' I cannot do as I once did, still I am happy!

My love to you and the clan—
Mary Youngchild

Tennessee Technological University
Cookeville, Tennessee

January 18, 2001

Mrs. Mary Youngchild
2489 Riverbend Rd.
Heber Springs, AR 72543-8657

Dear Mrs. Youngchild:

You are spot on! Computers are indeed in! They are the heartbeat of my workplace—the universe, actually! Endless potential!

Your extended trip abroad sounded exciting. Gloria and I cannot wait for a time when can attend the Grand Slam events in tennis—Wimbledon, French, Australian, US. Up to this point, our careers and the girls have been our primary focus. I sense that our turn for fun abroad will eventually come.

Most cordially,
Leo McGee
Associate Vice President for Academic Affairs

May 10, 2001

Dear Leo and Gloria,

Talked to B. last week—She is quite a gal and constantly amazes me. I was in Crossett about 24 hrs—left at 1:30 Saturday.

Philander Smith has been getting a lot of news space lately—gifts etc.—I forgot to cut it out before I passed my LRock paper on to a neighbor.

I'm teaching myself a lot about the computer and loving it. Never did anything like this before—wish Howard had lived to have one.

Love to the girls and you—M.

From: Leo McGee <lmcgee@tntech.edu>
To: MARY MEEK YOUNGCHILD marymyng@arkansas.net
Sent: Friday, June 01, 2001, 3:11 PM
Subject: My Mother

Mrs. Youngchild,

My mother seems to be extremely happy in the Pine Bluff Nursing Home. She is always laudatory about the food and activities there—social activities, church services, etc. She's amazing. My sister, Bobbie, sees her every day. My mother has been back to Crossett at least once. She wanted to see her house and visit friends. She accomplished both. Health wise, she is much, much better. Eating the right food and having excellent mental stimulation have made the difference.

We are planning a family reunion at the end of the month. We are all looking forward with great anticipation to this event, especially my mother.

                                                        Cordially,
                                                        Leo

From: MARY MEEK YOUNGCHILD <marymyng@arkansas.net>
To: Leo McGee <lmcgee@tntech.edu>
Sent: Saturday, June 02, 2001, 11:17 AM
Subject: My Mother

Dear Leo,

I was thinking of calling your mother today, and the first thing I saw on the e-mail was your letter re: her health and attitude. God bless her! The last time I spoke with her she seemed so happy. I am glad she was able to get back to Crossett once, and I know the reunion will be a real high for her. They broke the mold when they made her. I have so many happy memories of our association.

I continue to do well—drive anywhere easily. My scoliosis gives me fits now and then, and my knees aren't too helpful, but on the whole, I am fine.

It hurts not to be able to get down and do yard work as I always did, but I have accepted the fact that if and when I do cheat a bit, I have to pay for it.

My love to you old folks with grandchildren. It is amazing how fast one gets promoted to the older generation.

Love to you both,
Mary Y.

From: Leo McGee <lmcgee@tntech.edu>
To: MARY MEEK YOUNGCHILD <marymyng@arkansas.ne>t
Sent: Friday, August 31, 2001, 9:05 AM
Subject: My Mother

Mrs. Youngchild,

My mother is doing great! She attended the family reunion the last of June in Crossett. She looked great—even several years younger! She only uses a cane. No wheelchair! She was the attraction of the reunion.

Her health is much improved. She attributes it to proper medical care, proper diet, and a stimulating environment. They keep her busy in the nursing home. Then there is my sister, Bobbie, or cousins who visit her each day.

Last weekend, she went back to Crossett to attend church. She loved that. My mother is a wonder woman.

Cordially,
Leo

From: MARY MEEK YOUNGCHILD <marymyng@arkansas.net>
To: Leo McGee <lmcgee@tntech.edu>
Sent: Friday, August 31, 2001, 10:31 AM
Subject: Great News about that dear Willie B!!!!

Dear Leo,

I have not called your mom for about six weeks I believe. I must do it this weekend. She constantly amazes me.

It has been a long, hot summer. I have not done the watering I should, and, at the moment, I am hoping that the clouds above are not teasing me, but are truly full of rain. Even at age 81, I love to water like the dickens. Watering my 300' front yard keeps me busy. I will not mow. I told Howard that when I was doing everything else. He didn't want to either, so I managed not to learn how. As I said, I would wash windows, but I would not mow.

I had my knees checked out this week. The doctor does not recommend surgery (thank the Lord) but he will have me work with a therapist to learn the proper exercises. I spent spring battling my scoliosis, and Leo, I am only 5'6" now. It is so strange to be short after being on the back row when photographed all these years. I am still standing straight, and not stooped. The back is better, but I have had to slow down to get more comfortable.

I often think of the old days in Crossett...and always your mom is in there. We had a friendship that I always felt was above the working relationship. There was always a feeling of affection between us.

I know that the family reunion must have been wonderful and I know B. enjoyed it as did those who love and respect her. I can still hear the little chuckle she had when she laughed.

I have not been to Crossett since January. Our church lost its minister, and I am Chairman of the Worship Committee and have the "job" of filling the pulpit with ministers each Sunday. We hope to get an interim minister and then our own. I have been at it since May and have things organized thru October.

My love to you and Gloria…hard to think of you two as grand-parents and that Jennifer as a doctor, not an ice-cream eating child I saw in Cookeville way back in the '80s.

I will be sending you a new e-mail address soon when I go onto the Cox Cable Network. The new modem is ordered and I hope to be online at the new speed next week. A friend in the church will install it for me. I am not trained at taking parts out of and putting them into a computer. I really enjoy using it and writing up things for the family. I am still amazed at the things I can do considering my lack of technical training.

Tempus Fugit.

With love,
Mary Youngchild.

From: Leo McGee <lmcgee@tntech.edu>
To: MARY MEEK YOUNGCHILD <marymyng@arkansas.net>
Sent: Saturday, November 24, 2001, 1:36 PM
Subject: My Mother in Hospital

Mrs. Youngchild,

    My mother has been in the Pine Bluff Hospital for over a week. She has a kidney infection. Her situation is not good. She is very ill and is in a lot of pain. Because of her other complications, the medication has not been very effective.

    Along with my siblings, our visitations have been staggered. We are hoping for the best.

Cordially,
Leo

From: MARY MEEK YOUNGCHILD <marymyng@arkansas.net>
To: Leo McGee <lmcgee@tntech.edu>
Sent: Saturday, November 24, 2001, 1:50 PM
Subject: My Mother in Hospital

Dear Leo,

Thank you for letting me know that Willie B is ill. I am so very sorry. I will get a card off to her address and hope that she is better by the time it gets there. I know that you are very worried because despite her cheery, happy way, her health has suffered as she has aged. I know that because I can feel it in my bones and she leads me ten years. I love B as much as a relative and remember the many ways she helped me thru the years. Her good sense and faith helped me thru some rough times

Please keep me posted, Leo. I want to hear about her tho' briefly so as not to be a bother.

My best to you, Gloria and the girls.
Mary Y.

From: Leo McGee <lmcgee@tntech.edu>
To: MARY MEEK YOUNGCHILD <marymyng@arkansas>
Sent: Saturday, November 24 2001, 1:57 PM
Subject: My Mother in Hospital

Mrs. Youngchild,

I am impressed by your quick response! E-mail is wonderful! I have a very important meeting in New Orleans in a few days. I will perhaps have to cancel.

I shall keep you posted. I had a very brief conversation with my mother this morning. She confirmed that she is not doing well. For her to say that, she is probably really suffering.

Cordially,
Leo

From: Leo McGee <lmcgee@tntech.edu>
To: MARY MEEK YOUNGCHILD <marymyng@arkansas.net>
Sent: Saturday, November 24, 2001, 5:32 PM
Subject: My Mother in Hospital

Mrs. Youngchild,

    Your last message came up blank. No narrative.

Cordially,
Leo

From: MARY MEEK YOUNGCHILD <marymyng@arkansas.net>
To: Leo McGee <lmcgee@tntech.edu>
Sent: Monday, November 26, 2001, 8:26 PM
Subject: My Mother in Hospital

Leo, I am sorry. What I wrote was the fact I had sent a card to your mother at the nursing home, and I didn't know whether your sister would pick up her mail there. If you have an address at the hospital, or if your sister has a computer with e-mail, please send it to me. I just found this letter from you. I missed it yesterday because it popped up way out of line. Guess I need to clean out my e-mails.

I continue to pray that B will conquer this as she has so many things. God bless her.

Lovingly,
Mary Youngchild

From: Leo McGee <lmcgee@tntech.edu>
To: MARY MEEK YOUNGCHILD <marymyng@arkansas.net>
Sent: Monday, December 03, 2001, 11:03 AM
Subject: My Mother in Hospital

Mrs. Youngchild,

My mother received your card. I saw it on her bulletin board in the hospital. She was delighted to have it read to her. I was in Pine Bluff for three days last week.

She has really been in pain—kidney infection and bone infection on her foot. Most of her pain has subsided, but she is quite weak. She will probably have quite a stint in the hospital. She is in relatively good spirits, however. Talked with her last evening.

I believe the name of the hospital is Jefferson Memorial Hospital. I do not know the address, however.

Cordially,
Leo

Dec. 12, 2001

Dear Leo and Gloria,

Thanks for keeping me in touch—Leo—I did enjoy hearing you on the phone. Talked with your niece, Sonya, at the hospital last night and sent my love to Willie B. She told me that B. was too weary to speak. I understood.

Love—M.

From: Leo McGee <lmcgee@tntech.edu>
To: "mary youngchild" <marymyng@cox-internet.com>
Sent: Tuesday, January 22, 2002, 10:01 AM
Subject: Mother's Condition

Mrs. Youngchild,

My mother's condition has gone up and down during the past few weeks. When she returned to the nursing home from her first visit to the Pine Bluff Hospital, they placed her in an unfamiliar area of the home so she could get therapy. She did not like that area at all. She missed being with her friends. She was depressed and refused to eat, declaring that she was ready to go home to be with Jesus. Her health deteriorated to the point that she had to be returned to the hospital—Intensive Care, eventually. She had to receive her food intravenously. Her condition eventually improved to the point that she was able to go back to the nursing home—yesterday.

She was upbeat upon her return—feeding herself and hoping to walk again. She is a bit stronger now. However, this morning, she refused to eat. Officials at the nursing home called Bobbie to come in to feed her. Bobbie informed me that she ate a small amount of oatmeal and drank a little orange juice. I hope she will eat lunch.

My mother has really had a hard time, and she is tired. Perhaps her spirit will improve now that she is back in familiar territory in the home—back with friends.

Cordially,
Leo

From: "mary youngchild" < marymyng@cox-internet.com>
To: Leo McGee <lmcgee@tntech.edu>
Sent: Wednesday, January 30, 2002, 12:08 PM
Subject: Art Show

Thank you for including me on the list for the Joan Derryberry Gallery. I spotted that picture which you and Gloria "sponsor" and think it is a story of the old South and possibly the not so old South. I remember people in the fields before the mechanized cotton picker and they were not all black. The woman who helps me here is white and worked in the Warren area on a farm until she ran away and got married. She is one of the hardest workers I have ever seen. She is in her forties, I believe.

The programs for the year appear to be and have been very interesting. I once dabbled at painting, but I came to the conclusion that the world would not lose a great painter should I cease.

My zip was wrong and they noted that on the invitation. It is 72543.

Good talk with Bobbie the day after B's birthday. I hope things continue well. I read an allegory today to the effect that life is like a roll of toilet paper, the older you get, the faster it goes.

On that cultural comment, I will close with best wishes for a thoughtful reception of the exhibit.

                                        Mary Youngchild

THIS IS MY FINAL CONVERSATION WITH
MY DEAR BEDRIDDEN MOTHER

Silence.

"Leo, I'm ready to go home," Babe said. Babe is what her children call her as well as family members.

"Babe, you can't go back home," I responded. "I have rented your house."

"I'm not talking about going to my house in Crossett," she quipped. "I'm talking about going home to be with Jesus." Silence. She continued, "I told Bobbie if she is coming over to this nursing home to try and feed me, she might as well stay at home because I'm not eating anymore." Silence. "All of my life I have tried to do whatever Jesus has asked me to do. Now he has me in all of this pain. Leo, my whole body is in pain. I just don't understand why Jesus is treating me this way... I'm really tired. I'm tired of all this pain." Silence. "My daddy died at ninety-two, my mother died at ninety-two, my sister died at ninety-two, I'm ninety-two and I'm ready to go home."

Silence.

From: Leo McGee <lmcgee@tntech.edu>
To: "mary youngchild" <marymyng@cox-internet.com>
Sent: Wednesday, February 06, 2002, 4:22 PM
Subject: Sad News

Mrs. Youngchild,

My mother passed away yesterday. The funeral is Friday at 2:30 at Campground AME Church. The funeral home is:

Cromwell Funeral Home
Highway 82 East
Hamburg, AR 71646
(931) 364-4737

Cordially,
Leo

From: "mary youngchild" <marymyng@cox-internet.com>
To: Leo McGee <lmcgee@tntech.edu>
Sent: Wednesday, February 06, 2002, 5:30 PM
Subject: Sad News

Leo, I just discovered your (5:10 PM) message. I am so very sorry, but we all know that she had a long and happy life. How much she meant to the people who knew her. I gathered from Bobbie and from you that she was reluctant to eat. She was ready to go, and now she will be with her beloved Lord.

I want to send a memorial to her church in the Crossett area. Is it the one where the service will be? If you will, send me a name and address when it is convenient so that I can do that. I was there when your sister married, but I am not sure about the name. It has been a long, long time.

My condolences to you and the family.

I loved Willie B.
Mary Youngchild

From: Leo McGee <lmcgee@tntech.edu>
To: "mary youngchild" <marymyng@cox-internet.com>
Sent: Wednesday, February 13, 2002, 3:55 PM
Subject: Sad News

Mrs. Youngchild,

    You should send your memorial to my mother's minister, who commutes from McGehee, AR.

Rev. Artis Owens
167 HWY 159
McGehee, AR 71654

The name of the church is Campground AME Church.

Cordially,
Leo

2489 Riverbend Road
Heber Springs, AR 72543
February 14, 2002

Dear Leo and Gloria,

I am sure that you miss Willie B. but that you are happy that she is at peace. It must have been very hard for you to know that she was suffering and to have her refuse food and help. I remember that she was always so cheerful, serious at times but always reasonable. She helped me a lot with problems. I had her to talk with, and since she was there so much, she knew my situation.

I will always miss B. because she was a special lady and had a very good family. You children reflected well the things she and your father taught.

I never knew your father like I did Willie B. I tried to get him to visit with me, but he was reluctant to do so often. I did have a good relationship with your Grandfather Lowe. I believe that is spelled correctly. He was a great guy as they say now. I knew your grandmother, too, but he was the talker in the group. I am sure you enjoyed him as a child, Leo.

I had called Cromwell yesterday and they were going to e-mail me the address of the minister, but before they did so, your letter arrived so that I have prepared a letter to him. The town of McGehee is spelled with a lot more letters than your name. Outlanders call it Mc-ge-hee, which they do not.

I know how proud you are of your branch of the family tree. The girls have followed their parents with education first, and I know how proud you are of them. I would be.

I am enclosing a copy of the obituary out of the *Little Rock Democrat/Gazette*. I thought you might like it if you didn't already have one.

My love to you two and the girls.
Mary Youngchild

From: Leo McGee <lmcgee@tntech.edu>
To: "mary youngchild" <marymyng@cox-internet.com>
Sent: Thursday, February 21, 2002, 11:52 AM
Subject: Someone Special

Mrs. Youngchild,

   Thank you for your kind letter regarding my mother. Indeed, she was a special lady. I'll miss her a lot. I got to know her a lot better after I became an adult. During my younger years, there was sibling competition for her attention. The dynamics changed a bit in later years. I will always have fond memories of the time I had alone with her.
   You were very dear to my mother. Whenever your name was mentioned, she would always light up—becoming aglow! I would rejoice with her because I knew she was happy—overflowing with joy. Your warmth penetrated her soul. She loved talking about you—you coming by the senior center to visit, your phone calls, your birthday cards, what you had done for her, how nice you were to her. On a personal note, I'd like to thank you, from the bottom of my heart, for the kindness you showed my mother for so many years.
   I now pray that my grief will soon be replaced by pleasant memories of the past.

Cordially
Leo

From: "mary youngchild" <marymyng@cox-internet.com>
To: Leo McGee <lmcgee@tntech.edu>
Sent: Thursday, February 21, 2002, 12:19 PM
Subject: Someone Special

Dear Leo,

I do thank you for your kind words. I had to shed a few tears in memory of my friend and our relationship. I am so glad she knew how much I cared for her and about her. I will always want to know how you, Gloria, and the girls and their families are doing. I guess I am a people person, and I hate to let go of any one I love. My address book is formidable and my Christmas list is long. I love to touch base with friends at least yearly.

Thank you again. I know those memories of your mother when you had time alone with her are dear to you. As ever,

Mary Youngchild

From: "MARY MEEK YOUNGCHILD" marymyng@cox-inter-net.com
To: "Dr. Leo McGee" lmcgee@tntech.edu
Sent: Friday, March 29, 2002 11:21AM
Subject: Is this your cousin???

Dear Leo,

I was sent this section of the *Crossett* Paper which was like the one in which you were written up a few years ago by Bill Norman. I saw the same spelling of your name and wondered if this gal is a relative of yours. If so, I will send you the article. She seems to have had a most interesting life.

All goes well here…spring may eventually get here in a week or two. The river is up and flowing, the early flowers got beaten up by the rain and/or snow we managed to get when it should have been earlier.

Deb is planning on building IF the plan she has can be done on what she wants to spend. It will depend. She may have to settle for less. She wants high ceilings tho' not too much floor space, but it all counts. I try not to offer too many constructive suggestions.

She is busy this Easter weekend working 12-hour shifts on Good Friday thru Easter Day. She will be weary when she comes in Sunday evening.

May you and yours have a very happy Easter. I know that Willie B will have since she is with her Lord.

With affection, Mary Y.

Dec. 11, 2002

Dear Leo and Gloria,

This is the time I usually wrote and had a letter from Willie B. I feel strange not knowing that she is in her own home as independent as always, even driving to the senior citizens center. She was an amazing lady with such ability to go on and on. God bless her.

I know that you miss her even more than I since she was the matriarch of the family. Golly, I am, too. I expect to make it into my 90s but I have no idea how far...or even if.

I am very happy to be alone with my cat, Sultan, and my own house. I suppose the girls are continuing the things they were doing. Is Jennifer through with her medical training and a practicing physician now? Time goes so fast when it is someone else's children.

Happy Christmas to you and all the family.

Mary Youngchild

From: "mary youngchild" <marymyng@cox-internet.com>
To: Leo McGee <lmcgee@tntech.edu>
Sent: Tuesday, January 21, 2003, 2:35 PM
Subject: Your Dear Mother's Birthday

Dear Leo,

I always think of B. on Jan. 21 and always will because that was her birthday. I came across a copy in "Documents" on my computer of the card I had made for her last year. I think of her often. She was a lady of sound sense.

I know that you miss her very much. I just wanted you to know that I remembered her today with love, too.

Best of all to you McGees. Mary Y.

From: Leo McGee <lmcgee@tntech.edu>
To: "mary youngchild" <marymyng@cox-internet.com>
Sent: Tuesday, February 04, 2003, 12:14 PM
Subject: Your Dear Mother's Birthday

Mrs. Youngchild,

Indeed, I do miss my mother a lot. I truly enjoyed her during her final days. She made me extremely proud of who she really was. I am also truly delighted that she had such an influence on my life—all of her children's lives. She was a fine human being who gave so much of herself and cared so much for others. I never knew she had so many dear friends.

I drove back to Crossett in October to check on our old home place out in the country. It is all grown up in pine trees. I hardly recognized it. Briefly, fond memories of my childhood days there surfaced. I also drove by both of your former homes. I recalled transplanting hydrangeas and helping you clear the building site for the new home. The new home still looks great. I remember how fascinated my mother was with your new home. She particularly liked the squirrels running around in the yard! Your new home dominated her conversations for quite a while.

Jennifer graduated from medical school and has nearly completed her five-year residency in general surgery at Tulane in New Orleans. Right now, she and her mother are planning for a March 15 wedding in New Orleans. Some days they are on the phone to each other three or four times. Gloria is finding that it is extremely difficult trying to assist with wedding plans at such a great distance. There will be a reception in Cookeville on Saturday, June 7.

Cassandra's daughter, Jordan, is in the first grade. Cassandra gave up the Knoxville Chamber of Commerce job to become the Community Relations Director for the largest architectural firm in the city. Gloria and I are still enjoying our work at Tennessee Tech University.

It is always a real joy hearing from you.

Cordially,
Leo

When it finally dawned on me I had received my last letter from Mrs. Youngchild, sadness oozed into my space. A bit of emptiness and sorrow followed—distraught, ailing. Over time, joy replaced all of it. I learned to appreciate the true value of instinctive human-itarianism, which she exhibited so freely on behalf of my mother and I. This warmhearted and caring behavior was empowering, liter-ally transforming my life and enriching my mother's by a millionth degree—an invaluable gift both of us received from her! I shall cher-ish and attempt to emulate her behavior for the rest of my days!

AFTERTHOUGHTS

I now know why my mother always insisted that I visit Mrs. Conner on our returns home. This was her inconspicuous means of conveying that people of her race could accomplish the unthinkable if only given a chance. It warmed her heart to convey this message through her flesh and blood. I now know that Mrs. Conner-Youngchild loved my mother and me. We loved her in return. This triadic union emanated from the heart. The warm human spirit that bonded us has been a tremendous blessing to me. Their love of me was indeed sustenance for my somewhat tattered soul. No comfort of this sort was ever forthcoming from my teachers nor my peers. Working in White Town was more fulfilling than just about anything in my life. It was a soothing alternative to my environment at Daniel. While in Mrs. Conner's yard, I did not have to contend with a barrage of debasing taunts. The liberal praises that came from my employer nourished my spirit in a manner that nothing else could. Those gestures were tremendously empowering. I have attempted to incorporate those qualities exhibited by my mother and Mrs. Conner-Youngchild as I live my life—affable, empathetic, caring, giving, supportive, understanding, and Godly.

When my mother informed Mrs. Conner that her baby daughter was getting married, she was as excited as we were. She honored our family in a very special way. To our great delight, she became a terrific wedding planner—an act of love and instinctive humanitarianism.

Mrs. Conner's husband, Mr. Bob, was attentive to my welfare too. He made sure I got summer jobs at the Paper Mill. He also intervened when the Local Draft Board sent a threatening letter to Philander Smith College to inform me to expect MPs to come to campus to pick me up and take me straight to basic training. This threat came about because I failed, as an eighteen-year-old, to check in with the Board. No one told me to—an act of love and instinctive humanitarianism.

I could not understand why Mrs. Conner loved her hydrangea shrubs so much. Blooms drooped and foliage wilted in the sweltering heat. Blooms had no fragrance. At the time, I vowed to never ever plant a hydrangea in my own yard. Now in my senior years, the Leo and Gloria McGee Hydrangea Garden consist of more than 350 plants. *Better Homes and Gardens* featured our garden in its special interest publication, *Country Gardens*, fall 2015. The roots of this accomplishment emanated from acts of love and instinctive humanitarianism during years gone by.

King Features Entertainment of New York produced a documentary from the McGee article, which appeared in *Good Housekeeping*, October 1984. LIFETIME Cable Network carried it—host, John Mack Carter, Editor-in-Chief. The three-day filming for the production had immediately followed the filming of Hillary Rodham Clinton in Little Rock. This significant achievement was ungirded by acts of instinctive humanitarianism by an academic mentor.

Willie B. Mcgee
1910–2002

Mary Meek Conner Youngchild
1920–2004

Leo Mcgee
1941–

EXPLORATORY TOPICS

Instinctive Humanitarianism Defined
Hope, Dreams, and Challenges of Those in Subservient Roles
Instinctive Humanitarianism as a Modus Operandi
Identifying Role Models Across Racial Lines
Requisites for the Drive to Succeed
Endearing Others through Personal Persona
Race Relations in the 1950s vs. 2020s
Friendship Across Racial Lines
Significance of Redemptive Behavior
Personal Acts of Instinctive Humanitarianism Across Racial Lines

ACKNOWLEDGEMENTS

During my career in higher education, my venture down the writing path took a few turns—proposals for grant acquisition, reports for accreditation, and academic treatises for tenure/promotion. Then there was an attempt at creative writing! This is where I intersected with colleague Laura Clemons. Laura was a writer in Public Affairs at Tennessee Tech. Sharing my novel attempts in this genre increased over time. The excitement and enthusiasm of my mentor energized me. I am deeply indebted to Laura for inspiring me and for overseeing this project.

Posthumously, I want to thank two individuals from the bottom of my heart. My mother, Willie B. McGee, was always by my side. I am most appreciative of her unconditional love and thoughtful advice. On my behalf, Mrs. Mary Conner Youngchild went far beyond the call of duty in not the best of times. Her exhibition of instinctive humanitarianism strengthened my core more than any could imagine. These two souls deserve much of the credit for who I have become.

I extend heartfelt thanks to my dear wife, Gloria. She continues to put up with my unusual writing routine. Then there are our two daughters, Cassandra and Jennifer. I would like to thank them for the love and support of their families.

ABOUT THE AUTHOR

Leo McGee was born in Crossett, Arkansas. He began working in the yard of Mrs. Mary Conner at the age of twelve. His mother was her housekeeper.

He entered college in 1959 as a student athlete. Football was his sport of choice. He began his professional career as a public-school teacher in Chicago and Columbus, Ohio. After three years on the job, Ohio State University beckoned him to do graduate study. There he earned the master's and PhD degrees. The institution summoned him to be assistant director and director of clinical experience in the College of Education. Then there was the position of curriculum chair at Tennessee State University. His OSU mentor, now president of Tennessee Technological University, insisted that he join him. There he spent thirty years before retirement. His current title is associate vice president and professor emeritus.

He has written/cowritten five books on subjects relating to African American studies, grant acquisition for classroom teachers, and regional Tennessee history. He has received honors from Philander Smith College, Ohio State University, Harvard University, University of Tennessee, and Tennessee Technological University.

CPSIA information can be obtained
at www.ICGtesting.com
Printed in the USA
LVHW051006030720
659565LV00001B/54